ICME-13 Topical Surveys

Series editor

Gabriele Kaiser, Faculty of Education, University of Hamburg, Hamburg, Germany

More information about this series at http://www.springer.com/series/14352

Milton Rosa · Ubiratan D'Ambrosio
Daniel Clark Orey · Lawrence Shirley
Wilfredo V. Alangui · Pedro Palhares
Maria Elena Gavarrete

Current and Future Perspectives of Ethnomathematics as a Program

Springer Open

Milton Rosa
Universidade Federal de Ouro Preto
Ouro Preto, Minas Gerais
Brazil

Wilfredo V. Alangui
University of the Philippines Baguio
Baguio
Philippines

Ubiratan D'Ambrosio
Universidade Anhanguera
São Paulo
Brazil

Pedro Palhares
Universidade do Minho
Braga
Portugal

Daniel Clark Orey
Universidade Federal de Ouro Preto
Ouro Preto, Minas Gerais
Brazil

Maria Elena Gavarrete
Universidad Nacional de Costa Rica
Heredia
Costa Rica

Lawrence Shirley
Towson University
Towson, MD
USA

ISSN 2366-5947
ICME-13 Topical Surveys
ISBN 978-3-319-30119-8
DOI 10.1007/978-3-319-30120-4

ISSN 2366-5955 (electronic)

ISBN 978-3-319-30120-4 (eBook)

Library of Congress Control Number: 2016934944

Printed on acid-free paper

This Springer imprint is published by Springer Nature
The registered company is Springer International Publishing AG Switzerland

Contents

Chapter 1
Introduction

Milton Rosa and Lawrence Shirley

Ethnomathematics as a program studies the cultural aspects of mathematics. It acknowledges that there are different ways of doing mathematics by considering the appropriation of academic mathematical knowledge developed by different sectors of the society as well as by considering different modes in which different cultures negotiate their mathematical practices (D'Ambrosio 2001). Ethnomathematics researchers investigate ways in which different cultural groups comprehend, articulate, and apply ideas, procedures, and techniques identified as mathematical practices.

These mathematical practices refer to forms of mathematics that vary as they are embedded in cultural activities. In this regard, "ethnomathematics can be characterized as a tool to act in the world" (Orey 2000, p. 250) since it provides insights into the social role of academic mathematics. It presents the mathematical concepts of the school curriculum in a way in which these concepts are related to the cultural backgrounds of students (D'Ambrosio 2001), thereby enhancing their ability to make meaningful connections and deepening their understanding of mathematics.

In this context, there is a need to examine the embeddedness of mathematics in culture, drawing from a body of literature that takes the students' cultural base of knowledge production into the mathematics curriculum (D'Ambrosio 1999). The field of ethnomathematics studies students' diverse ways of knowing and learning as well as culturally embedded knowledge in the pedagogical action of this program. Ethnomathematics explores the interaction of academic and cultural ways to provide inclusive developmental programs for diverse populations served by educational institutions. This program includes curricular relevance and builds curricula around the local interests and culture of the learners (Rosa and Orey 2015).

The main foundation of an ethnomathematics program is an awareness of the many ways of *knowing and doing* mathematics that relates to the values, ideas, notions, procedures, and practices in a diversity of contextualized environments. In this regard, we have come to recognize the need to consider the appropriation of academic mathematical knowledge in different societal contexts as well as ways in which members of distinct cultural groups negotiate their own mathematical

M. Rosa et al., *Current and Future Perspectives of Ethnomathematics as a Program*, ICME-13 Topical Surveys, DOI 10.1007/978-3-319-30120-4_1

practices (D'Ambrosio 2001). Teaching mathematics through cultural relevance and personal experiences helps students to know more about reality, culture, society, environmental issues, and themselves by providing them with mathematics content and approaches that enable them to master academic mathematics successfully. An ethnomathematics approach to the curriculum is considered a pedagogical vehicle for achieving such a goal (Rosa and Orey 2007).

Ethnomathematics represents the way that various cultural groups mathematize their own reality because it examines how both mathematical ideas and mathematical practices are processed and used in daily activities. It is described as the art and techniques developed by students from diverse cultural and linguistic backgrounds used to explain, understand, and manage social, cultural, environmental, political, and economic environments (D'Ambrosio 2007). It provides us with a research paradigm that is much wider than the traditional concepts of mathematics, ethnicity, and multiculturalism, where *ethno* is related to distinct groups identified by cultural traditions, codes, symbols, myths, and specific ways of reasoning and inferring. This program seeks to study how all learners understand, comprehend, articulate, process, and ultimately use mathematical ideas, concepts, procedures, and practices to solve problems related to their daily activities.

This holistic context helps students to reflect, understand, and comprehend extant relations among all of the components of the system. Ethnomathematics is at the heart of instructional methodologies. Therefore, it is necessary to prepare students to work in a diverse, multicultural world, with recognition of the contributions the members of other cultural groups have made to mathematics (Shirley 2001) and with an appreciation and openness to new and alternative perspectives, paradigms, and worldviews. In this regard, detailed studies of the mathematical ideas and practices of distinct cultural groups most certainly allow us to further our understanding of the internal logic and mathematical ideas of diverse group of students. This program is aware of diverse ways of knowing and doing mathematics: the ideas, notions, procedures, and practices contextualized in distinct environments. In this regard, we have come to recognize the need to consider the appropriation of academic mathematical knowledge in different societal sectors as well as ways in which members of distinct cultural groups negotiate their own mathematical practices (D' Ambrosio 2001).

In this context, the main objective of this *ICME-13: Topical Survey* of *TSG35: Role of Ethnomathematics in Mathematics Education* is to show that ethnomathematics provides mathematics education with an important framework that can help transform mathematics into a discipline that is better able to contribute to the attainment of the dream of an equitable and humane society. In this regard, "mathematics is powerful enough to help us build a civilization with dignity for all, in which iniquity, arrogance, violence, and bigotry have no place, and in which threatening life, in any form, is rejected" (D'Ambrosio 2004, p. IX).

Similarly, it is important to understand that diverse sociocultural representations and concepts of *ethno* develop from distinct ideas, procedures, practices, and dimensions of space and time through the relationship between group members in different cultural environments. This can be done by conducting research on how investigations based on ethnomathematics contribute to a different perspective of the very nature of mathematics, which includes valuing and examining the relationship among different mathematical systems.

Chapter 2
An Overview of the History of Ethnomathematics

Ubiratan D'Ambrosio

To discuss perspectives is to reflect on our wishes, goals, and actions, which are all in the present. In order to do that, we rely on past experiences; thus, the present is the interface between past and future. Before reflecting on perspectives, I will recount some moments of my trajectory in ethnomathematics. My first participation in an International Congress on Mathematical Education was in the 1976 ICME 3, in Karlsruhe, Germany. I consider the ICME 3 a milestone in Mathematics Education. Many mathematics educators at the Congress raised concerns about issues that were beyond mere content. Many proposals for study groups, among which were the History and Pedagogy of Mathematics (HPM), Political Dimensions of Mathematics Education (PMDE), and the Psychology of Mathematics Education (PME), were launched at the ICME 3.

The program of the ICME 3 was organized through survey papers that reported the perceptions of mathematics educators around the world on crucial issues. I was invited to be in charge of the survey paper for Section B-3: "Overall Goals and Objectives for Mathematics Education: Why Teach Mathematics?" In the survey paper I prepared, I contended that the "primary objective of mathematical education is not to perpetuate knowledge or to push existing knowledge further, which will go on or fade away, but to foster the creation of new knowledge." Now, 40 years later at the ICME 13 in Hamburg, Germany, I reflect on these same issues and claim that the role of mathematics educators goes beyond teaching academic mathematics content. Their role is to foster students' creativity, even if this requires some insubordination in conducting their classroom practices.

In order to prepare the Survey Paper for Section B-3, I proposed a critical discussion of the Western-centric history of mathematics. I also discussed how Western mathematics played an essential role in building modern civilization. Western mathematics is the essential tool for economy, finances, and marketing and is the root of modern capitalism. It remains closely related to politics, social stratification, religion, and ideology. It was essential for the great navigations as well as conquest and colonization. In this process, Western mathematics subdued and even eliminated other models of civilization. My concerns were in agreement with some of my colleagues and in disagreement with others.

© The Author(s) 2016
M. Rosa et al., *Current and Future Perspectives of Ethnomathematics as a Program*, ICME-13 Topical Surveys, DOI 10.1007/978-3-319-30120-4_2

To create new knowledge we have to look to society as a whole and to its constitutional cultural dimensions, taking into account the traditions and expectations of its members. In that survey paper, I emphasized essential ideas of a critical view of Western-centric mathematics. I criticized the fact that the mainstream image of mathematics education focused mainly on the transmission of mathematical content, with less attention given to social justice and cultural issues. This critique was the essence of what would become the ethnomathematics program. However, it was also a proposition for a new view of the history and philosophy of mathematics and their pedagogical implications.

The state of the world today is serious. There is an increasing demand for education in every small country, and ethnomathematics can contribute to addressing a number of the global challenges school systems face. Ethnomathematics is more acceptable to native populations and more accessible and affordable, mainly for those living both in rural and coastal areas. It appeals to traditional practices; hence, it is more attractive than the sometimes cold and austere formal mathematics in their existing programs.

This is also true in more developed areas, where services are a mix of traditional practices for common needs that rely on specialized workers and artisans, such as builders and maintenance people in general, as well as on more specially trained professionals in areas of universal interest and reach, such as commerce, industry, and technical services. These needs all rely on what people are doing in their everyday life. This is the basic component of ethnomathematics, which should be an option and a choice offered by a well-functioning school system that balances ethnomathematics and official school mathematics. The two systems need not clash and can blend in harmony. There may be an effective improvement in school mathematics, but also improvement of ethnomathematics, which may receive valuable contributions from theoretical reflections offered by academic mathematics.

In his famous conference of 1900, David Hilbert said:

> History teaches the continuity of the development of science. We know that every age has its own problems, which the following age either solves or casts aside as profitless and replaces by new ones. ... not only invites us to look back into the past but also directs our thoughts to the unknown future. (Hilbert 1900 cited in Reid 1996, p. 74)

Hilbert was referring to academic mathematics, but the same remarks are also true for ethnomathematics and indeed for every system of knowledge. History shows that the evolution of academic mathematics reflects the changes of many factors, particularly cultural ones, including linguistic, social, political, economic, ideological and religious factors.

The same is true for the evolution of ethnomathematics, which is as dynamic as academic mathematics in its evolution and reflects the same set of factors. The complexity of situations and problems that determined the generation of traditional ethnomathematics have changed, so the solutions proposed must also change. We have to recognize that new methods and new facts will be absorbed and incorporated by ethnomathematics in the same way that they are by academic mathematics and any system of knowledge.

There is a misconception, which I call a romantic view, that ethnomathematics has been preserved as it originated with our ancestors. Ethnomathematics is dynamic and changes very fast. Indeed, it is less conservative than academic mathematics. As long as new facts, phenomena, situations, and problems require ethnomathematical solutions, ethnomathematics will be alive. A lack of evolution of ethnomathematics foreshadows extinction, and the cessation of its development may give it characteristics of folklore.

Ethnomathematics is dynamic, holistic, transdisciplinary, and transcultural. Its evolution surely will benefit academic mathematics, mainly because ethnomathematics advances in a way that is much closer to reality and to the agents immersed in reality. The agents of academic mathematics are usually encaged in their ivory towers, as denounced by Mikhail Gromov:

> I would not only focus on mathematics but on science and art and whatever can promote creative activity in young people. When this develops, we may have some influence but not before that. Being inside our ivory tower, what can we say? We are inside this ivory tower, and we are very comfortable there. But we cannot really say much because we don't see the world well enough either. We have to go out, but that is not so easy. (Raussen and Skau 2010, p. 403)

We need to modernize the rich resources and cultural heritage of both ethnomathematics and academic mathematics and put them in their proper position in today's world. The history of ethnomathematics is a flourishing field, richer than the history of mathematics, as it relies significantly on non-written sources.

I recall what happened after ICME 3. The word ethnomathematics was never used in my survey paper. As a matter of fact, the word had never occurred to me. In 1977, in the annual meeting of the AAAS in Washington DC, Rayna Green organized a session on Native American knowledge. I gave a talk in the session and I used the word *ethno-mathematics*, in the narrow sense of the mathematics of indigenous populations. I was influenced by the use, mainly by anthropologists, of the words *ethno-musicology*, *ethno-botany*, *ethno-linguistics*, and other words used for ethno-disciplines. I was unaware that the word had been used before by educators under the influence of anthropologists.

Although the use of the word ethno-mathematics as the mathematics of other ethnic groups still prevails in mathematics education, I went further to question the meaning of both the prefix *ethno-* and the word *mathematics*. I realized that the prefix ethno- is much broader that ethnic. It means a culturally identified group sharing knowledge and practices, language, and myths. Indeed, what many ethnomathematicians are doing is looking for ethnic-mathematics, which is contradictory. The nature, history, and philosophy of mathematics have shown how inappropriate it is to look for mathematics in different ethnic groups, as well as in different ethnos or cultures.

Mathematics, as understood in schools and academia, is an organization of concepts generated and developed in the Mediterranean Basin. Such concepts have been organized since the Lower Middle Ages and the Renaissance as a discipline that was called mathematics. This discipline was the base for the development of powerful modern science and technology. Modern science and technology, which is based on mathematics, were the most successful instruments in the development of capitalism and in the process of conquest and colonization, which subjected the entire world to Western civilization. This led me to reexamine the concept of mathematics, its nature, its history, and its philosophy and pedagogical implications. These were the basic ideas that were organized in preparing the opening plenary conference of ICME 5 in 1984 in Adelaide, Australia, when I used the word ethnomathematics in the broad sense of *tics of mathema in distinct ethnos* (D'Ambrosio 1985).

How did I conceive the word ethnomathematics in this sense? It is a personal story of etymological construction. Some colleagues say it is an etymological abuse! In 1978, I participated in the International Congress of Mathematicians in Helsinki, Finland. In this Congress, I was recognized for helping to increase the number of participants from developing countries and for proposing a satellite conference on the day preceding the opening of the ICM on Mathematics and Society. A large number of participants attended this session, which was not an official event of ICM 1978.

In Finland, I embraced fantasy. The great Norwegian mathematician Sophus Lie said that, "Without fantasy, I could never become a good mathematician." While in that country, I was curious about the rich mythology of the indigenous peoples living in the Arctic territories and their strategies for survival and transcendence. How do these people deal with their natural and sociocultural environment? How do they recognize and explain the facts and phenomena present in their lives? I speculated on how the Finnish people would express, in their language, the strategies for survival and transcendence of the indigenous populations.

Such strategies always imply understanding, explaining, learning, and dealing with the natural and sociocultural environment. I like to play with dictionaries. When go to different countries, I usually buy a small dictionary and use much of my free time to browse through it. In 1978, while in Helsinki, I bought an English-Finnish-English Dictionary. Finnish is a very difficult and strange language. I played with my little dictionary and composed a word with Finnish roots to express the ways, arts, and techniques developed by the indigenous peoples to understand, explain, and learn about the facts and phenomena of their natural and sociocultural environment. The result was *alusta-sivistyksellinen-tapas-selitys*! Or, to make it a little less frightening: *alustapasivistykselitys*. Impossible!

Using Greek roots might make my etymological wordplay easier as well as create a less shocking word to express the same idea. Browsing a well-known classical Greek etymological dictionary, I found three interesting words: *techné* (for ways, arts, and techniques), *mathemá* (for understanding, explaining, and learning), and *ethno* (for a group within the same natural and sociocultural environment that has compatible behavior). These roots combined would make for *techné* of *mathemá* in an *ethno*. A little modification gives *tics* of *mathema* in different *ethnos* and a different ordering gives *ethno-mathematics*. Obviously, *ethnomathematics*, the word which resulted from my theoretical reflection about the origins and evolution of knowledge of the human species, is a more acceptable word to express both the reality of indigenous cultures and the fantasy of a mythological legend.

Each culture develops ways, styles, and techniques for doing things as well as responses to the search for explanations and the quest for understanding and learning, or essentially how and why we do things. In the human species, early attempts to explain and understand led to the search for origins, which led to myths. These attempts were organized as systems of knowledge and religions. The attempts to explain and understand rely on observation, comparison, classification, evaluation, quantification and measurement, counting, representation, and inference, which are steps in the generation of knowledge. Western mathematics is such a system of knowledge, as shown by an overview of its history. Thus, I decided to analyze the origins and evolution of Western mathematics as a system of knowledge in the broader sense of the responses to the need for survival and transcendence, taking into account practical and mythical motivations.

In response to their own environments, other cultures have also developed other systems of knowledge with the same objective. We might refer to such systems as "other mathematics," each of which uses a different way of observing, comparing, classifying, evaluating, quantifying and measuring, counting, representing, and inferring. All of the different knowledge systems that resulted from an effort to cope with different environments should be called ethnomathematics. They are all motivated by the drive for survival and transcendence and are compatible with their myths, religions, and language. Although similar reactions may occur in different natural and cultural environments, each context has its own responses, that is, its own ethnomathematics. This led me to try to understand the origins and evolution of systems of knowledge in general, looking into their entire generation cycle, intellectual and social organization, and diffusion of knowledge as well as the subsequent changes in the systems that resulted from the cultural dynamics of encounters.

Encounters presuppose the presence of the human species all over the planet. Whether we consider our species to have a single primeval origin or multiple origins, the mobility of pre-historic humans and consequent encounters of groups of different genetic backgrounds, coming from different natural and sociocultural environments and different mythological traditions, is undeniable. The encounters, which are motivated by many reasons such as territorial disputes, search for natural resources, mythical motivation, commercial exchanges, and conquest wars, result in the mutual exposition to different genetic structures, different cultures, and different knowledge systems. Such diverse reasons for the encounters are not isolated, the boundaries between them are not clear, and they all interfere with each other. We cannot analyze one single reason. They all have mutual implications and a holistic historical analysis is necessary.

The historiography of the dynamics of encounters is very complex. The mutual exposition of knowledge systems, in a broad sense, may result in various degrees of assimilation, subordination, and even suppression of a system of knowledge. What occurs in most cases is a syncretism of ways of doing and knowing, as well as ideas, which gives rise to new systems of knowledge. Every encounter reveals ideological conflicts, and it is impossible to completely remove the traces of assimilated or suppressed systems. Extant traces are always present and identifying them is a great challenge for research. We might call this research *paleography of ideas*.[1]

A broad view of the history of mathematics, focusing on anthropological, social, political, religious, and other issues as well the cultural dynamics of encounters, is a very clear illustration of the full cycle of knowledge. It looks into how the processes of observing, comparing, classifying, evaluating, quantifying, measuring, counting, representing, and inferring originated in different cultures. It also examines how cultural dynamics played an important role in the development of these forms of knowledge, leading, as a result, to local institutionalization and local ways of thinking and doing.

Geopolitics determined that the Greek language and philosophy had a marked influence in Mediterranean antiquity. The word mathematics, present in the several versions in Classical Greek as well as in Latin, has different meanings. It was only in the early Renaissance that the word mathematics came into use with a meaning similar to the one used today: a science in itself, detached from philosophy and from other sciences that appropriates concepts and techniques from various branches of philosophy from earlier times and many different cultures.[2]

It is common to use of the word ethnomathematics to refer to a specific indigenous culture. As stated above, this is deceiving. It is a mistake to look to a particular cultural environment for ideas and categories of knowledge that are appropriate to a different cultural environment. It is clear that in each different culture we have to look into the ways, arts, and techniques that were developed to express their understanding, to explain and learn about the facts and phenomena of their natural and sociocultural environment, and, consequently, their ways of doing and knowing.

I hope the synthesis above explains current and future perspectives of the research program that I call the *ethnomathematics program*.

---

[1]The full cycle of knowledge and the cultural dynamics of these encounters is explained in D'Ambrosio (2000).

[2]According to etymological dictionaries, the word *mathematics* in the modern sense used nowadays appeared only after the 15th century.

Chapter 3
State of the Art in Ethnomathematics

Milton Rosa and Daniel Clark Orey

Ethnomathematics uses the etymology of three Greek roots, *ethno, mathema*, and *tics*. It is a program that incorporates mathematical ideas and procedures practiced by the members of distinct cultural groups, which are identified not only as indigenous societies but as groups of workers, professional classes, and groups of children of a certain age group as well (D'Ambrosio 1985).

This program is concerned with the motives by which members of specific cultures (*ethno*) developed, over history, the measuring, calculating, inferring, comparing, and classifying techniques and ideas (*tics*) that allow them to model natural and social environments and contexts in order to explain and understand these phenomena (*mathema*).

In order to understand the development of ethnomathematics as a program, it is necessary to discuss its current and future perspectives as well as to analyze its goals, objectives, and assumptions regarding the encouragement of the ethics of respect, solidarity, and cooperation among cultures. Thus, this survey on the state of the art of ethnomathematics addresses themes related to ethnomathematics and its six dimensions and diverse pedagogical approaches, which deal with issues of culturally relevant pedagogy, innovative approaches, and the role of this program in mathematics education.

3.1 Six Dimensions of Ethnomathematics

Over the past three decades, a significant amount of research in ethnomathematics has been developed by a large number of researchers in Brazil and other countries. In this regard, ethnomathematics represents a methodology for ongoing research and analysis of the processes that transmit, diffuse, and institutionalize mathematical knowledge (ideas, processes, and practices) that originate from diverse cultural contexts through history. This context enabled the development of the six important dimensions of the ethnomathematics program: Cognitive, Conceptual, Educational,

© The Author(s) 2016
M. Rosa et al., *Current and Future Perspectives of Ethnomathematics as a Program*, ICME-13 Topical Surveys, DOI 10.1007/978-3-319-30120-4_3

Epistemological, Historical, and Political. These dimensions are interrelated and aim to analyze sociocultural roots of mathematical knowledge.

(a) Cognitive

This dimension concerns the acquisition, accumulation, and dissemination of mathematical knowledge across generations. Thus, mathematical ideas such as comparison, classification, quantification, measurement, explanation, generalization, modeling, and evaluation are understood as social, cultural, and anthropological phenomena that trigger the development of knowledge systems elaborated by the members of distinct cultural groups. In this regard, it is not possible to evaluate the development of cognitive abilities apart from social, cultural, economic, environmental, and political contexts.

(b) Conceptual

The challenges of everyday life give members of distinct cultural groups the opportunity to answer existential questions by creating procedures, practices, methods, and theories based on their representations of reality. These actions constitute a fundamental basis for the development of essential knowledge and decision-making processes. Survival depends on immediate behavior in response to routines inherent to the development of the members of the group. Thus, mathematical knowledge emerges as an immediate response to the needs for survival and transcendence.

(c) Educational

This dimension does not reject knowledge and behavior acquired academically, but incorporates human values such as respect, tolerance, acceptance, caring, dignity, integrity, and peace into the teaching and learning of mathematics in order to humanize it and bring it to life. In this context, ethnomathematics promotes the strengthening of academic knowledge when students understand mathematical ideas, procedures, and practices present in their daily lives. Therefore, a "practice and presentation of mathematics, critically and historically grounded ... may resist cooptation and be prone to be used for humanitarian and dignifying purposes" (D'Ambrosio 2009, p. 266). These are the main ideas of *nonkilling mathematics* as proposed by D'Ambrosio in his search for peace and transcendence.

(d) Epistemological

This dimension deals with knowledge systems, which are sets of empirical observations developed to understand, comprehend, explain, and deal and cope with reality. Thus, three questions arise regarding the evolution of mathematical knowledge in relation to diverse forms of generation, organization, and dissemination: (a) how to move from ad hoc observations and practices to experimentation and methods, (b) how to move from experimentation and method to reflection and abstraction, and (c) how to proceed towards inventions and theories. These questions guide reflections regarding this evolution by considering the unique interplay between people and their own reality.

(e) Historical

It is necessary to study links between the history of mathematics and the reality of the learners. This dimension leads students to an examination of the nature of mathematics in terms of the understanding of how mathematical knowledge is allocated in their individual and collective experiences. Thus, knowledge is constructed from the interpretations of ways humanity has analyzed and explained mathematical phenomena throughout history. This is why it is necessary to teach mathematics within a historical context so students are able to understand the evolution of and the contributions made by other peoples to the ongoing development of mathematical knowledge.

(f) Political

This dimension aims to recognize and respect the history, tradition, and mathematical thinking developed by the members of distinct cultural groups. The recognition and respect for the sociocultural roots of these members does not imply the rejection of the roots of *others*, but reinforces these roots through dialogue in cultural dynamism. It also aims to develop political actions that guide students in transition processes from subordination to autonomy in order to guide them towards a broader command of their rights as citizens.

These dimensions show that the ethnomathematics program has an agenda that offers a broader view of mathematics that embraces ideas, processes, methods, and practices that are related to different cultural environments. This aspect leads to increased evidence of cognitive processes, learning capabilities, and attitudes that may direct the learning process occurring in our classrooms. In addition, reflecting on the dimensions of this program reveals that another important aspect of its agenda is to offer an important perspective for a dynamic and globalized modern society that recognizes that all cultures and all people develop unique methods and explanations that allow them to understand, act, and transform their own reality.

3.2 Ethnomathematics and its Diverse Pedagogical Approaches

Lawrence Shirley and Pedro Palhares

Even before ethnomathematics emerged as a field of study, mathematics teachers were looking to culture to find examples to use in their classrooms. Many ethnomathematicians of today started as teachers who became excited to find cultural connections for their pedagogical work. Ethnomathematics provided enrichment and new topics that students had not seen before, demonstrating that mathematical applications can be found not only in many areas of science, business, and everyday life, but also that we can see mathematics in cultural practices around the world. In addition, it has often been pointed out that ethnomathematical examples demonstrate new ways of looking at mathematics and lead to a better understanding of the concepts, procedures, and uses of curricular content.

With this obvious link between ethnomathematics and classroom practice, it is almost superfluous to describe ethnomathematics and the pedagogy of mathematics education. However, this is being offered as both background and foundation for discussions at the study group on ethnomathematics at the Thirteenth International Congress on Mathematical Education. It is hoped that the review of examples of ethnomathematics in the mathematics classroom will stimulate further discussion and encourage more classroom applications of ethnomathematics.

When the International Study Group on Ethnomathematics was established, four general areas of interest were identified: (1) field research, where data about mathematics in culture is collected; (2) mathematical work in cross-cultural situations; (3) classroom applications of ethnomathematics; and (4) theoretical, sociological, and policy studies of ethnomathematics. Obviously, the third area is the main theme of this chapter, which will look at pedagogical examples, a few of which will be given later on. Nonetheless, the other three areas of interest also strongly feed into the pedagogical uses of ethnomathematics.

In some cases, ethnomathematical data collected can be translated almost directly into curriculum material, content for enrichment, activities based on cultural uses of mathematics, and new applied examples for students to work with. Even if not directly applicable, any classroom use will depend on information learned from field research. Wide distribution of research results should help teachers who may be seeking new material for their classes.

Considerable ethnomathematical experience emerges from teachers working with students of another cultural group, or living away from their home culture. Any diligent mathematics teacher needs to learn about the culture of their students and make the mathematics content relevant to local interests. This might require changes in approach to the content or even instructional techniques. Ethnomathematical work with policy issues might include lobbying for more diversity in school curricula, including more cultural background material in mathematics pedagogy. This includes making mathematics lessons attractive and valuable to underrepresented groups in the increasingly diverse populations of many countries of the world. It has even been suggested that the encouragement of objective thinking in mathematics translates into political action in oppressive societies. Thus, teaching mathematics becomes a subversive activity!

It almost seems obligatory to begin with the example of Claudia Zaslavsky, a classic early case of a school teacher turned ethnomathematician. She was a secondary mathematics teacher in New York City in the 1960s. Her son was working in a teaching program in Tanzania, where she visited him. Like all good teachers, she always kept alert for anything to use in her classes. In Tanzania, she saw gesture counting, mankala games, and other local applications of mathematics.

Later, she visited several other parts of Africa searching for more examples of mathematics in African culture. After consulting with several experts, she brought her examples and commentary together in her book *Africa Counts* (Zaslavsky 1973), which became a popular resource for teachers in the United States, Africa, and elsewhere. Over the following years, she continued to produce articles and books, all aimed at using cultural examples in mathematics teaching; a few are included in the bibliography.

African culture provides many examples for ethnomathematics in the classroom, beyond even counting and games. Many traditional symbols, artwork, and sculptures demonstrate bilateral and circular symmetries, and many incorporate geometrical shapes. Textile art, especially in West Africa, can be used to show more symmetry and patterns, while loom and weaving technology itself is a good example of engineering mathematics. Incidentally, textile art is also present in many other parts of the world: Navajo blankets from Arizona, USA; tartan patterns from Scotland, UK; costumes from Bali and Indonesia; etc.

With appropriate study, any one of these can be translated into classroom applications, especially the study of patterns and symmetry. We can also draw examples from communities based on a particular professional activity. There are many examples, such as the study carried out by Gerdes (2005) on artifacts production in Mozambique and its application in mathematics education or the study of fishing communities including boat construction by caulkers (Palhares 2012). A great number of professional activities have already been studied, such as foremen, masons, or folk dancers.

Ron Eglash, an important ethnomathematics researcher, who bases his work partially on West African content, has conducted a great deal of formal research on actually offering this content for classroom use and with individual students, especially in the development of the computer software called *Culturally Situated Design Tool*, which allows students to create and modify patterns from traditional culture on their own. Babbitt et al. (2015) report a quasi-experiment (rather rare in pedagogical research), comparing the use and non-use of Ghanaian *Adinkra* designs in teaching junior high mathematics. The *Adinkra* patterns are discussed within their cultural context and translated into software design programs.

This experiment showed significant improvement for classes using cultural connections. Eglash et al. (2011) and Babbitt et al. (2012) picked up on Eglash's earlier work (1999), which found fractal patterns in the design of several aspects of West African culture such as jewelry, hairstyles, and city planning. This was also developed into computer software for classroom use. In this study, the content also included examples of Native American design patterns. Students can manipulate parts of the design, notably showing the self-repeating patterns of fractals.

Similarly to Zaslavsky, Gerdes, Eglash, and others who wrote about African mathematics, other areas of the world have also been included in mathematics pedagogy through ethnomathematical applications. An early reporter of ethnomathematics in the Americas is Luis Ortiz-Franco. Over two decades ago, he described examples of Hispanic ethnomathematics (Ortiz-Franco 1993), including examples in historical context and daily life. Later, he broadened his viewpoint to include other cultures of the Americas (Ortiz-Franco 2002). The Aztecs are especially known for their large circular calendar, but the process of developing the calendar and other mathematical aspects of their historical culture led to an interesting counting system, as well as astronomy and algebraic thinking for problem solving.

Several ethnomathematicians have written about the use of Native American mathematics in classrooms. Ascher (1991) and Rauff (2009) noted the very accurate applications of probability in Iroquois games, which can be played in mathematics classes. Barta and Shockey (2006), working in the western part of the United States, found good cultural examples from the Northern Ute people, which were especially relevant as they could be used directly with Native American (including Ute) students. Similarly, Herron and Barta (2009) describe actual culturally appropriate applications in second-grade classrooms. Much farther north, in Alaska, the mathematics of the Yup'ik people connected with time, distance, and direction was used in designing new school curricula (Engblom-Bradley 2006).

Another way of looking at it comes from the work of Brousseau (1997), who claims that mathematicians, when communicating mathematics, tend to depersonalize and remove both context and temporal marks. This is an important objective in formal mathematics, as it enables the achievement of generality and abstraction. Teachers, however, have to give meaning to mathematical content, so they have to personalize, contextualize, and inscribe it temporally. This is what Brousseau (1997) called didactic transposition. Some believe that ethnomathematics, the mathematics of identifiable cultural groups (D'Ambrosio 2006), can help in this process of contextualization and, furthermore, the humanization of mathematics (Palhares 2012).

One can also look at the concept of numeracy, which viewed from a cultural point of view, is very close to an ethnomathematics approach as both focus on culturally-situated practices (Rosa and Orey 2015). Similar to the trend in science teaching, which currently distinguishes the learning of the experimental data-gathering practices of scientists from scientific theory, Bishop (2010) proposes that the school mathematics curricula should be designed in a way that deals with ethnomathematics practices (numeracy) and mathematical theory as two separate but related strands.

When examining educational applications of ethnomathematics it may be useful to recall studies made about learning in out-of-school situations and how it may help us in the pedagogy of mathematics education. For Nunes (2010), people who learn mathematics outside school build their learning on the understanding of situations rather than on algorithmic learning and are also more versatile in their reasoning schemes.

More importantly, people develop this kind of versatility in situations which make sense to them. She then suggests that mathematics education should focus on the development of mathematical models for reasoning rather than on arithmetic operations. The teaching of operations should be used as an instrument that is secondary to problem solving rather than as the starting point for problem solving.

Based on anthropology, Bishop (2002) introduces the concepts of enculturation (when young people get to know their own culture) and acculturation (when another culture is introduced) and maintains that mathematics teachers can be seen both as mathematics enculturators and acculturators. If teachers are attempting to *correct* the way students think in order to make them reasonable people who reason in specific ways, then they are preparing them to be governed by systems of power and authority. Fostering students' awareness of the mathematical vocabulary and supporting them in developing their own ways to succeed may be viewed as empowerment of students; pedagogy is therefore not value-free (Appelbaum et al. 2015).

The project led by Bill Barton and colleagues took this direction and for quite a number years aimed at expanding Maori language so that mathematics could be taught in Maori, thus not only empowering students in class but theoretically as a whole community (Barton et al. 1998). This led to a series of issues, namely the balancing between language fossilization (as it cannot be used in advanced studies and therefore will be abandoned) and corruption of language (as its development is brought about from an already fixed meaning in English). However, Barton (2008) claims that new mathematical ideas lie hidden in minority languages and urges that they be developed.

An interesting example is the location system, which in the dominant view of mathematics is achieved either by the Cartesian coordinate system or the polar coordinate system, both with a single point of origin. But the Tahitian and Maori languages, when locating an object, use two points of origin, the speaker and the listener, and two angles, one at each of the origins. This can be developed into a mathematically valid system. Barton's global conclusion on this point is that each language contains its own mathematical world. As to pedagogical implications, he stresses the need for formal language development within the mathematics curriculum and the need to teach about the nature of mathematics. One other interesting suggestion is that undirected mathematical play (at some point he calls it *mathematical gossip*) is a good idea at all levels of education, from kindergarten to university.

The arguments often given for using ethnomathematical examples in classrooms are (a) to show students of underrepresented cultures that their own cultures do contribute to mathematical thinking and (b) to expose students of majority cultures to different cultures from around the world, building respect for others and generally contributing to global education. These are certainly laudable goals. However, occasionally ethnomathematicians have expressed concern that too often Western field research tends to seek the *other* to the extent of exploiting indigenous cultures. One possible way to avoid this problem and, notably, bring the goals of ethnomathematics even more directly to students, is to encourage students to do ethnomathematical studies of their own individual cultures, heritage, and personal interests (Shirley 2015).

If students make presentations to each other, they all learn about all of the cultures represented in the classrooms. Students from underrepresented groups can demonstrate the contributions of their groups. Examples can come from family traditions, hobbies, religions, and occupations; geography-based activities; celebrations of holidays and life events; personal interests such as sports, music, art, dance, or crafts; and even child-related activities, from playground games and computer games to skateboarding, jumping rope, and birthday parties. All bring the students' attention to cultures, and all show applications of mathematics. Mathematics is everywhere!

3.3 Innovative Approaches in Ethnomathematics

Milton Rosa and Daniel Clark Orey

Ethnomathematics offers a broader view of mathematics that embraces ideas, notions, procedures, processes, methods, and practices rooted in distinct cultural environments. This aspect leads to increased evidence of cognitive processes, learning capabilities, and attitudes that direct learning processes occurring in classrooms. In addition, by reflecting on the social and political dimensions of ethnomathematics, another important aspect of this program is the possibility for the development of innovative approaches for a dynamic and *glocalized society*. *Glocalization* is the acceleration and intensification of interaction and integration among members of distinct cultural groups.

Ethnomathematics also recognizes that such members develop unique techniques, methods, and explanations that enable alternative understanding, comprehension, new actions, and transformation of societal norms. At the same time, the theoretical basis of an ethnomathematics program is growing as a valid alternative to traditional studies of the historical, philosophical, cognitive, and pedagogical aspects of mathematics. Thus, the research program for ethnomathematics is broadening its theoretical basis with the diversity of new investigations as innovative approaches and frameworks are produced and implemented (Rosa 2014).

It is necessary to discuss and debate interrelated innovative approaches in ethnomathematics programs, such as their relation to social justice, civil rights, indigenous education, professional contexts, game playing, urban and rural contexts, ethnotransdisciplinarity, ethnopedagogy, ethnomethodology, ethnomodelling, and ethnocomputing. The trivium curriculum for mathematics proposed by D'Ambrosio (1999) is an important innovative ethnomathematics approach that needs more investigation in order to address pedagogical purposes.

3.3.1 Social Justice

Many researchers in ethnomathematics investigations would agree that an emphasis on education for social justice is paramount. It is increasingly necessary to empower students by teaching them about real-world issues and instill in them a desire to seek out and work towards their goals. Students who do not believe in, value, or recognize their own cultural roots can easily assimilate the dominant culture without critically reflecting on its values (D'Ambrosio 1999).

Thus, it is extremely necessary to contextualize mathematics, as knowledge emerges from the needs and expectations of the members of communities that come to use it. Teaching for social justice through ethnomathematics focuses on the context of the understanding of mathematical ideas, procedures, and practices developed by members of these communities, which forces confrontations in relation to assumptions about *truth* and *knowledge*, and which can easily be confused with the *right* and *wrong* in mathematics.

This environment shows that information may be meaningless unless it is embedded in appropriate contextual understanding. Thus, social justice relies on the relevant political and cultural aspects of mathematics in order to mediate instruction and encourage exploration, interpretation, and reevaluation of how humanity conceives the nature of mathematics.

However, it is important to emphasize that usually mathematical processes are not easily altered for teaching social justice considerations. There are, of course, exceptions, especially within the field of ethnomathematics, that use different methods of organizing mathematical ideas, procedures, practices, and problem solving that explore how members of different cultures organize and classify knowledge. In this context, when the focus of a study is the pedagogy of mathematics, the attention must be focused both on legitimizing students' knowledge that originates from experiences built in their own ways and on the study of pedagogical possibilities of how to work with the learning processes that occur both outside and inside the school environment.

Indeed, a discussion of the educational aspects of ethnomathematics helps teachers establish cultural models of beliefs, thought, and behavior. This can be done by contemplating the potential of pedagogical work that both takes into account the sociocultural background of students and provides a more meaningful and empowering mathematical learning experience. The suggestion of starting with a student's existing mathematical concepts is another way to provide a more critical examination of such concepts.

The consequence of this approach for teacher education is quite significant. It means that teachers must know more about the mathematics and additional pedagogical competencies of their community in order to help students undertake a critical and reflective examination of mathematical knowledge. In this regard, teaching is considered a higher order task that helps researchers, teachers, and students understand the connection between mathematics and culture.

Mathematics for social justice has to be equal for students from different cultural backgrounds. An important change in mathematics instruction needs to take place in order to accommodate social and cultural changes in society. Therefore, teachers need to have support that enables them to gear education towards students from distinct cultures.

3.3.2   Ethnocomputing

In 2002, Tedre introduced the term *ethnocomputing* in his dissertation entitled *Ethnocomputing: A Multicultural View on Computer Science* at the University of Joensuu in Finland (Eglash et al. 2006). Ethnocomputing is the study of interactions between computers and the cultural knowledge that emerges from the members of distinct cultural groups. It is a research field that studies computing applications in different cultural settings. Thus, ethnocomputing offers a tool for developing a multicultural approach in computer science education as it recognizes the influence of social and cultural backgrounds on computing technology (Tedre 2002).

In this context, ethnocomputing research has its roots in ethnomathematics. For example, an early investigation conducted by Ascher and Ascher (1981) of the Inca Quipus and the study developed by Eglash (1999) on African fractals are two of the first examples of the application of ethnocomputing (Tedre 2002). However, a decade earlier the results of the study conducted by Petrillo (1992) showed a connection between computing and cultures as an autonomous research field. In his study entitled *Ethnocomputers in Nigerian Computer Education,* Petrillo (1994) reworked the concept of ethnocomputing developed in his doctoral dissertation entitled *Responsive Evaluation of Mathematics Education in the Community of Jos in Nigeria* (Petrillo 1992).

By applying the concept of ethnocomputing, Eglash et al. (2006) uncovered mathematical knowledge embedded in the designs of various characteristics of native and contemporary cultures, from traditional beadwork and basket-weaving to modern hairstyles and music, by using culturally situated design tools consisting of web-based software applications that allow students to create simulations of cultural arts.

Ethnocomputing places mathematics in the heritage identity of students in order to recover their hidden computational capital by developing a series of interactive, web-based teaching tools that capture their interest and imagination in mathematics classes. Thus, the application of "…ethnocomputing results in an expressive computational medium that affords new opportunities to explore the relationships between youth identity and culture, the cultural construction of mathematics and computing, and the formation of cultural and technological hybridity" (Eglash et al. 2006, p. 347).

In this regard, it is necessary to make real-world connections that tie into the students' cultural heritage in the process of teaching and learning mathematics. Culturally situated design tools provide a flexible learning environment to do that, which enables students to reconfigure the relationship between cultures, mathematics, and technology.

3.3.3   Ethnomodelling

In 2002, Bassanezi introduced the term *ethno/modelling*[1] by arguing that mathematical ideas, procedures, and practices used in daily life present alternative interpretations of reality. In the ethnomodelling approach, the use of ethnomathematics assumptions and the application of tools and techniques of mathematical

---

[1]The term ethno/modelling comes from a book by Bassanezi (2002) entitled *Ensino-aprendizagem com modelagem matemática* [Teaching and learning with mathematical modelling]. In this manuscript the term ethno/modelling was adapted to ethnomodelling.

modelling allow us to perceive reality by using different lenses, which gives us insight into mathematics performed in a holistic way (Rosa and Orey 2013).

Therefore, modelling provides a valuable pedagogical approach suitable for an ethnomathematics program because it contextualizes mathematical knowledge developed locally. Thus, ethnomodelling is the study of mathematical phenomena that occur in diverse cultural contexts. These phenomena are socially rooted constructs that include the cultural aspects of mathematical knowledge in the modelling process.

Ethnomodelling is the process of elaboration of problems and questions that grow out of practical contexts and form an image or sense of idealized versions of *mathema*, which are the actions for explaining and understanding daily phenomena in order to survive. The focus of this perspective constitutes a critical analysis of knowledge generation and production (creativity), so we are able to discuss the social mechanisms of the institutionalization of knowledge (academics) and its transmission through generations (education) (Rosa and Orey 2010).

It also presents a set of educational opportunities developed through the modelling process conducted in sociocultural contexts. Such contexts allow the critical exploration of local mathematical knowledge by appreciating and respecting cultural values developed by members of distinct cultural groups. This stance indicates that mathematical knowledge is inherent to the reality of these members. This knowledge establishes itself as a tool for the decision-making process regarding their unique perspective and reality (Rosa and Orey 2013).

The holistic context created by analyzing reality as a whole allows students to engage in the modelling process in order to study reality systems in which there is an equal effort to create an understanding of all aspects and components of the system studied as well as the interrelationships among them (D'Ambrosio 1990). Such systems have revealed sophisticated mathematical ideas and procedures that include, for instance, the geometric principles in craftwork and architecture and the traditional practices encountered in activities and artifacts found in local contexts.

Such mathematical practices involve numeric relations found in measuring, classification, calculation, games, divination, navigation, astronomy, modelling, and a wide variety of other mathematical procedures used in the production of cultural artifacts (Eglash et al. 2006). This context allows the development of a definition of ethnomodelling as the translation of local mathematical ideas, procedures, and practices, in which the prefix *ethno-* relates to the specific mathematical knowledge developed by the members of distinct cultural groups. Thus, it is necessary to start with the social context, reality, and interests of the students and not merely enforce a set of external values and decontextualized curricular activities which have no meaning for them (Rosa and Orey 2013).

In this regard, the main aspect of the ethnomodelling approach is not just to solve problems nor to understand alternative mathematical systems. This approach also helps students gain a better understanding of the importance and role of mathematics in society (Araújo 2010; Barbosa 2006).

3.3.4 *Trivium Curriculum*

The trivium curriculum for mathematics is composed of *literacy*, *matheracy*, and *technoracy* and enables the development of school activities based on an ethnomathematics and modelling foundation.

Literacy is the ability students have to process and use information present in their daily lives by applying reading, writing, representing, and calculating techniques as well as using diverse media and the internet (D'Ambrosio and D'Ambrosio 2013). From an ethnomathematical perspective, literacy is the integration of the cultural contexts of the school and the community through cultural dynamism, which allows students to exchange academic and local knowledge.

In the modelling perspective, teachers guide students to select a topic through dialogue and discussion. Themes are very general in nature, and allow students to engage in mathematical exploration and creativity. The implementation of mathematical modelling precedes an ethnographic investigation of mathematical systems found in the school community (Rosa and Orey 2015).

Matheracy is the ability students have to interpret and analyze signs and codes in order to propose models to find solutions for daily problems. It provides symbolic and analytic instruments that help students develop creativity and allow them to understand and solve new problems and situations (D'Ambrosio and D'Ambrosio 2013). In an ethnomathematical perspective, matheracy is the domain of skills, strategies, and competencies that empower students to be aware of the way in which they explain their beliefs, traditions, myths, symbols, and scientific and mathematical knowledge.

In a modelling perspective, matheracy is the ability to interpret, manipulate, and handle signs, symbols, and codes as well as to propose the elaboration and use of mathematical models in everyday life. This approach allows students to have access to a diverse set of codes and symbols, which are essential in the decision-making process for the elaboration of mathematical models (Rosa and Orey 2015).

Technoracy is the ability students have to use and combine different technological instruments that help them solve problems they encounter in everyday activities in order to assess the reasonableness of the results and their contextualization (D'Ambrosio and D'Ambrosio 2013). From an ethnomathematical perspective, technoracy is an important feature of scientific knowledge as well as its reification as technological artifacts. It can manifest itself in technological tools that translate ways of dealing with natural, social, cultural, political, and economic environments.

Such environments facilitate the incorporation of diverse modes of explanation, belief, tradition, myth, and symbols in the development of mathematical knowledge. In the modeling process, technoracy is the incorporation and use of diverse tools that include calculators, computers, software, computational programs, and simulators.

Frequently, the technological tools used in specific sociocultural contexts unleash the development and elaboration of mathematical models (Rosa and Orey 2015). This curriculum model provides educators with a "critical way, with the communicative, analytical, and technological instruments necessary for life in the 21st century" (D'Ambrosio and D'Ambrosio 2013, p. 22). The incorporation of the trivium into classrooms implies a curricular reconceptualization in which ethnomathematics and mathematical modelling are tools for pedagogical action.

3.3.5 Some Considerations

Currently, there is growing awareness about the understanding and comprehension of mathematical ideas, procedures, and practices developed by the members of distinct cultural groups. This is primarily due to the expansion of studies related to culture, history, anthropology, linguistics, and ethnomathematics. Discoveries made through the ongoing investigations of the many and diverse theoretical and empirical studies show that it is possible to internationalize mathematical practices that emerge in different cultural contexts.

An important characteristic of ethnomathematics is the transformational power it has to help rethink the nature of mathematics. This means that one possible purpose for ethnomathematical studies and their innovative approaches could be to foster the development or transformation of mathematics. We hope that these innovative approaches of ethnomathematics will provide a better understanding of this research program.

3.4 Polysemic Interactions between Ethnomathematics and Culturally Relevant Pedagogy

Milton Rosa and Maria Elena Gavarrete

Over the past three decades, the theoretical bases for ethnomathematics (D'Ambrosio 1985) and culturally relevant pedagogy (Ladson-Billings 1995) have sought to ease sociocultural concerns as part of an examination of the cultural and socioeconomic influences on the processes related to teaching and learning mathematics. This includes knowledge, as well as a commitment to challenging social injustice, and reflections upon educational challenges involving identifying obvious and subtle individual, institutional, and cultural actions that perpetuate social structures.

The overall goal of this theoretical base is to empower students through learning activities that help them develop literacy, numeracy, and technological, social, and political skills in order to be active participants in a democratic society. It is important to emphasize that investigations conducted regarding culturally relevant pedagogy study the cultural congruence between the backgrounds of students, communities, and schools, which in turn form one of the main principles of an ethnomathematics program (Hart 2003).

This means that cultural congruence indicates the respect teachers have for the social, cultural, and linguistic backgrounds of students. Educators (both the school management and teachers) must gain knowledge of and develop respect for the diverse cultural traditions, languages, prior mathematical knowledge, and respective community contexts of their students so that they are able to implement the principle of cultural congruence in schools and classrooms.

Mathematics tends to be presented as a set of objective and universal facts and rules; it is commonly viewed as *culture free* and not considered a socially and culturally constructed discipline. In order to change this perception, it is necessary that curriculum developers and teachers take into account what is considered mathematics and how this knowledge relates to the norms and values of diverse cultures (Rosa 2014). If, as educators, we come to integrate the diverse cultures we encounter in our school communities, then there is a need to create a conceptual framework to make coherent decisions regarding curricular activities concerning the mathematics curriculum.

3.4.1   Ethnomathematics and Culturally Relevant Pedagogies in Teacher Education

An important change in mathematical instruction needs to accommodate continuous and ongoing changes in students' demographics in mathematics classrooms around the world. Since ethnomathematics proposes that educators contextualize their mathematics teaching and learning by relating mathematical content to the sociocultural experiences of their students, it has become necessary to integrate culturally relevant pedagogies and diverse ethnomathematics perspectives into existing teacher education programs.

The guidelines of the National Council of Teachers of Mathematics (NCTM 1991), the Brazilian Ministry of Education and Culture (Brasil 1997), and the Ministry of Public Education (Costa Rica 2012) highlight the importance of building connections between mathematics and the sociocultural contexts of students. Thus, when students are encouraged to examine mathematical activities in their own sociocultural contexts, they realize that mathematics procedures and practices are not trivial, as they see them connected to their daily lives (Rosa and Orey 2007). In this perspective, students may succeed in mathematics when their understanding of it is linked to real and meaningful cultural referents and when instruction assumes that all students are capable of mastering mathematics (Ladson-Billings 1995).

Curricular activities developed according to principles of culturally relevant pedagogy focus on the role of mathematics in sociocultural contexts. These activities involve ideas and procedures associated with ethnomathematical perspectives to solve problems. In this approach *ethno-* is defined as a culturally identifiable group with its own jargon, codes, symbols, myths, and even specific ways of reasoning and inferring; *mathema* is defined as categories of analysis; and tics is defined as methods or techniques for solving daily problems (Rosa and Orey 2013).

The inclusion of cultural aspects in a mathematics curriculum has long-term benefits for students' mathematical achievements, as these aspects contribute to the perception that mathematics is part of our daily lives and deepen the understanding of its nature by enhancing students' ability to make meaningful connections. Pedagogical work towards an ethnomathematics perspective allows for a broader analysis of school contexts in which pedagogical practices transcend classroom environments (Rosa 2014).

Ethnomathematics presents possibilities for educational initiatives and new curriculum objectives based on culturally relevant pedagogies. However, one dilemma regarding this issue is how to prepare teachers to create curriculum activities based on culturally relevant pedagogies and ethnomathematics (Greer 2013). One approach to solve this dilemma is to focus on the importance of promoting the dissemination of heritage aspects of local, cultural, and mathematical knowledge in order to help students strengthen their own cultural identities in school environments (Gavarrete 2014). It then becomes necessary to list a number of assumptions that prevail in mathematics education regarding Eurocentric perceptions found in the development of mathematics.

This approach shows that there is a need to encourage reflection about the development of mathematics in distinct cultures as well as the need to include ethnomathematics in teacher training processes in order to elevate pedagogical actions and combat the exclusion promoted by monocultural perspectives in the mathematics curriculum. Educational monocultural perspectives distort or limit the educational process of ethnomathematics, especially in indigenous contexts, because textbooks and other curricular materials have given little attention to non-representant, non-mainstream cultures in rural areas (Gavarrete 2012).

For example, it is necessary to study the mathematical knowledge developed by the members of Ngäbes, Bribris, and Cabécares ethnic groups in Costa Rica in order to propose pedagogical actions for teacher education programs pertaining to their worldview and particular logical traditions. The respect for the ideas and procedures implicit in social practices will provide prospective teachers with pedagogical tools that help them conduct teaching and learning processes in a contextualized fashion (Gavarrete 2012).

In this regard, it is necessary to propose a discussion about cultural relevance in teacher education programs in order to help prospective teachers acknowledge the relationship between cultural and school mathematical knowledge. This approach also fosters a reflective attitude about the universality and contextualization of mathematical knowledge, since pedagogical work with ethnomathematics promotes teacher creativity when developing a mathematics curriculum that is connected to the sociocultural environment of the students.

3.4.2 Culturally Relevant Activities Based on Ethnomathematics: Curricular Implications

Ethnomathematical approaches are intended to make school mathematics more relevant and meaningful to students in order to increase the overall quality of education and assert more culturally relevant views of mathematics. The application of any culturally relevant pedagogies and accompanying ethnomathematical perspectives in classrooms validates and incorporates the cultural background resulting from the ethnic heritage of students as well as their current interests into the daily instructional practices of teachers. It empowers students intellectually, socially, emotionally, and politically by using their sociocultural and historical realities and contexts to convey knowledge, impart academic skills, and change students' attitudes towards academic instruction (Ladson-Billings 1995).

This pedagogical approach is achieved through dialogue when community members, teachers, and students discuss mathematical themes that help them work on problems that are directly relevant to their community. In this context, students investigate conceptions, traditions, and mathematical practices developed by members of distinct cultural groups in order to incorporate them into the mathematics curriculum. Below we share two examples that demonstrate the kind of development found in culturally relevant activities in order to explore ethnomathematical relationships between ideas, procedures, and practices developed by the members of distinct communities.

(a) Measuring land

The use of the practice of cubic content calculation (cubação) as a pedagogical proposal to elaborate activities for the teaching and learning of mathematics shows the importance of the contextualization of problems in the learning environment through the connection of ethnomathematics and culturally relevant pedagogy concepts. In this regard, Knijnik (1997) proposed activities related to the demarcation of land from research work with the members of Movimento dos Trabalhadores Rurais Sem Terra (MST)[2] in Southern Brazil.

The land demarcation activity involved a method for calculating cubic content, which is a traditional mathematical practice applied by the members of this movement. It concerns the solution of problems of measuring irregular-shaped land. Figure 3.1 shows how to calculate an area of land with a quadrilateral shape measuring 114 m $\times$ 152 m $\times$ 90 m $\times$ 124 m.

Thus, the mathematical knowledge developed by the members of Movimento dos Trabalhadores Rurais Sem Terra presents a model that transforms the shape of the given plot of land into a rectangle (Fig. 3.2) whose dimensions are 138 m by 102 m with an area of 14,076 m^2.

---

[2]Movimento dos Trabalhadores Rurais Sem Terra (MST), the "Landless Rural Workers Movement," is a social movement in Brazil whose purpose is to fight for the redistribution of land to poor workers in general.

Fig. 3.1 Land with an
irregular quadrilateral shape

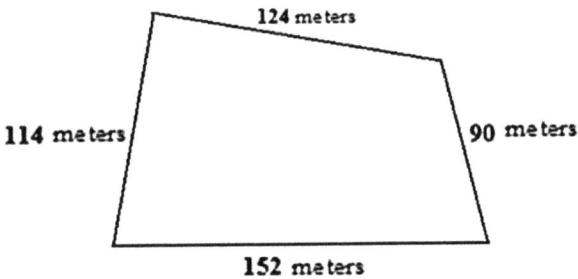

Fig. 3.2 Land with a *regular rectangular shape*

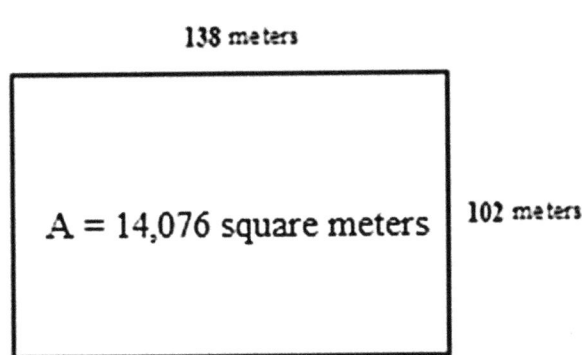

The following model explains this mathematical practice:

- Transform the irregular quadrilateral shape into a rectangle whose area can be determined through the application of the formula $A = b \cdot h$.
- Determine the dimensions of the rectangle by calculating the mean of the two opposite sides of the irregular quadrilateral.

$$\text{Base} = \frac{152 + 124}{2} = 138 \, \text{m}$$
$$\text{Height} = \frac{114 + 90}{2} = 102 \, \text{m}$$

- In order to find the area of this irregular quadrilateral, it is necessary to determine the area of the rectangle.

$$A = b \cdot h$$
$$A = 138 \cdot 102$$
$$A = 14{,}076 \, \text{m}^2$$

There is yet another model developed by the members of Movimento dos Trabalhadores Rurais Sem Terra that explains this mathematical practice. The members of this cultural group transform the irregularly shaped quadrilateral into a square with 120-m sides, which has an area of 14,400 m². Thus, the measure of 120 m was calculated by adding the dimensions of the quadrilateral and then dividing it by four, which is the number of sides of the irregular quadrilateral (Rosa and Orey 2013).

(b) Mathematization of the tipi

Spatial geometry is inherent to the shape of the tipi and it was used to remind, indeed symbolize, the universe in which the Plains People lived. The Sioux language word tipi refers to a conical skin tent common among these North American tribes. Through history, the nomadic prairie people observed that the tripodal foundation appeared to be perfectly adapted for harsh environments.

There is evidence that Sioux people had an understanding of the characteristics and properties of geometry concepts such as triangles. For example, the majority of Sioux tribes use a three-pole foundation (Fig. 3.3) because it is stronger and offers a firmer foundation for the tipi (Rosa and Orey 2013).

The base of the tipi formed by the three-pole foundation is the triangle ABC (Fig. 3.4). The midpoints of each of the sides of $\triangle$ABC are points M, N, and P. It is possible to match each vertex of $\triangle$ABC to the midpoint of each opposite side, which gives us the straight lines AM, BN, and CP.

These straight lines form three medians, which are the straight lines connecting the midpoint of each opposite side of the triangle to its vertex. The medians intersect at one single point called the centroid. Archimedes demonstrated that the medians of a triangle meet at its balance point or center of gravity, which is the centroid of the triangle. Native Americans place their fire and altar at this point in the Tipi because it "holds a definite power and holiness" (Orey 2000, p. 246).

(c) Classification as a mathematical activity in indigenous contexts

Classification is an essential activity in some indigenous communities. Examples of cultural mathematical knowledge (CMK) show that indigenous people possess a holistic sense of reality that allows them to establish a conceptual structure in which relationships between the world and its tangible and intangible objects are understood, connected, and represented. Therefore, CMK is associated with classification systems practiced through oral tradition, and it uses metaphorical and symbolic logic that is applied to the study of ethnic groups whose cosmogony includes other representational systems such as the physical and symbolic mythical worlds (Gavarrete 2015).

For example, classification of linguistic systems of three Chibchan indigenous groups has been studied linguistically within an ethnomathematical perspective in Costa Rica. These oral indigenous languages use numeric classification to identify objects that are arranged or counted according to geometric shapes used in their daily lives, such as long, flat, and round (Gavarrete 2015).

In the particular case of the Cabecar language, the numeric metaphor sa'jula refers to the five fingers of a hand to represent the number five. Thus, in general,

Fig. 3.3 Three-pole
foundation of the tipi

Fig. 3.4 Triangle *ABC*,
which forms the base of the
tipi

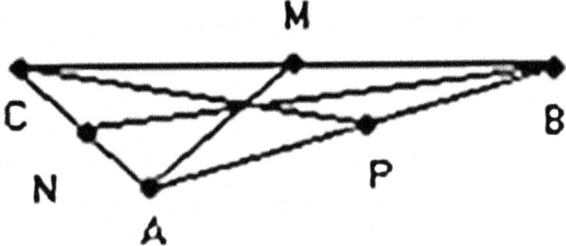

multiples of five relate to flat classification because the palm of the hand is flat, but when numbers are not multiples of five or objects have shapes other than flat, a combination of numeric classifications is used (Gavarrete 2012).

This specificity regarding classification systems in the indigenous communities of Costa Rica demands a reflection on the lack of contextualized academic resources and about the pedagogical challenge of teaching arithmetic in a culture that applies diverse systems of numeric classification that differ from academic mathematics used in schools (Gavarrete 2013).

3.4.3 Some Remarks

The objective of developing a mathematical curriculum based on ethnomathematics and culturally relevant pedagogies is to help students become aware of how people mathematize and think mathematically in their own cultures and to use this awareness to learn about formal mathematics, and increase their ability to mathematize in any context in the future. Students also come to value and appreciate their previous mathematical knowledge, which allows them to understand and experience these cultural activities from a mathematical point of view, thereby allowing them to make the link between school mathematics and the real world. An ethnomathematical curriculum helps students understand the nature of mathematics because it presents them with an effective tool that can contribute to their learning of mathematics (Rosa and Orey 2007).

The integration of ethnomathematics and culturally relevant pedagogies into the mathematics curriculum focuses on the development of this research area as a process rather than a collection of facts, as it is based on the idea that mathematics is a human creation that has emerged as people attempt to understand and comprehend the world around them. Therefore, mathematics can be seen as a rich and diverse cultural process and a human activity rather than just a set of academic content (Rosa 2014).

Mathematics knowledge in the context of a culturally relevant pedagogy is perceived in an ethnomathematical perspective because teachers build from the students' informal mathematics and direct the lesson toward their culture and experiences while developing their critical thinking skills. This environment allows us to reflect on the nature of mathematics, culture, education, and society and the relationships among them in order to include pedagogical practices in the teaching and learning of mathematics that address deeper notions of equality (Gavarrete 2014).

Therefore, we reiterate the importance of promoting a sociocultural approach in the mathematics curriculum in order to combat the curricular decontextualization resulting from a monocultural view. However, this approach faces the challenge of transcending ethnocentrism and enriching the process of teaching and learning mathematics through the incorporation of ethnomathematics and culturally relevant pedagogy into teacher education programs.

3.5 Role of Ethnomathematics in Mathematics Education

Wilfredo V. Alangui and Milton Rosa

Ethnomathematics as a program came to prominence in the opening speech by Brazilian educator Ubiratan D'Ambrosio at the 1984 Fifth International Congress on Mathematics Education in Adelaide, Australia, in order to problematize the relations between mathematics, culture, and society. This program has brought together mathematicians and mathematics educators who have different motivations for their pursuit of ethnomathematics under several international organizations such as the International Study Group on Ethnomathematics (ISGEm) and the Ethnomathematics Working Group of the International Conference on Mathematics Education (ICME).

Since 1984, five international conferences on ethnomathematics (ICEm) have already been held in Spain (1998), Brazil (2002), New Zealand (2006), United States (2010), and Mozambique (2014). These conferences have attracted ethnomathematicians and educators from over 20 countries, illustrating the growing geographical scope of ethnomathematics. Brazil remains the leading country in terms of ethnomathematical activity and is the only one that has held four national congresses on ethnomathematics.

In the last three decades there has been a large amount of research, investigations, theses, and dissertations that deal with theoretical and practical aspects of ethnomathematics. At the same time numerous articles, book chapters, and books were written about the relationship between culture, mathematics, and mathematics education. During these decades, studies involving ethnomathematics were discussed and debated in a succession of local, regional, national, and international meetings, seminars, conferences, and congresses.

These congresses and conferences show that mathematics education research in the field of ethnomathematics has been both active and evolving in many parts of the world. In addition, they also show a variety of approaches, which has led to different conceptions of ethnomathematics. Thus, it is important to show here an overall perspective on the theorical basis of ethnomathematics by presenting a survey on the role of ethnomathematics in mathematics education.

3.5.1 Survey on the Role of Ethnomathematics in Mathematics Education

In order to understand the holistic context of ethnomathematics, this survey focuses on the papers produced in Brazil from 2005 to 2014 as well as those presented in the last three ICEm congresses in 2006, 2010, and 2014, which were categorized according to the six dimensions of ethnomathematics originally proposed by D'Ambrosio (2006).

Table 3.1 Ethnomathematics production in Brazil from 2005 to 2014

Dimensions	Epistemological	Historical	Educational	Political	Cognitive	Conceptual
Master	11	9	40	10	15	14
Doctorate	5	6	15	5	9	11
Total	16	15	55	15	24	25

(a) Brazilian production in ethnomathematics

A total of 150 doctoral dissertations and master theses from three official Brazilian agencies and 25 research groups in mathematics education were analyzed in this survey. Articles, book chapters, books, and proceedings were not investigated due to the large amount of ethnomathematics production in Brazil. Table 3.1 shows Brazilian ethnomathematics production from 2005 to 2014.

(b) International production in ethnomathematics

A total of 123 papers including plenaries, parallel sessions, and posters from three international congresses on ethnomathematics were analyzed in this survey: 31 from ICEm3, 42 from ICEm4, and 50 from ICEm5. Tables 3.2, 3.3, and 3.4 show ethnomathematics production in the ICEm 2006, 2010, and 2014 congresses.

The data shows that the Educational dimension has been the most predominant in ethnomathematics production (36.3 %) over the last 10 years, which

Table 3.2 Ethnomathematics production in the ICEm5—Maputo, Mozambique, 2014

Dimensions	Epistemological	Historical	Educational	Political	Cognitive	Conceptual
Presentations	4	4	16	2	5	8
Plenaries	2	1	3	1	2	2
Total	6	5	19	3	7	10

Table 3.3 Ethnomathematics production in the ICEm4—Baltimore, United States, 2010

Dimensions	Epistemological	Historical	Educational	Political	Cognitive	Conceptual
Presentations	6	2	9	1	4	7
Plenaries	1	–	–	2	–	1
Posters	–	–	5	1	1	2
Total	7	2	14	4	5	10

Table 3.4 Ethnomahematics production in the ICEm5—Auckland, New Zealand, 2006

Dimensions	Epistemological	Historical	Educational	Political	Cognitive	Conceptual
Presentations	3	1	10	1	2	7
Plenaries	2	1	1	1	–	2
Total	5	2	11	2	2	9

demonstrates its importance for mathematics education. This survey also demonstrated that it is necessary to include issues regarding the use of knowledge developed by the members of specific cultural groups and the connections with pedagogical actions of this program.

However, discussions surrounding these issues did not imply that ethnomathematics is only an instrument needed to improve mathematical education because it also takes on important roles in helping clarify the nature of mathematical knowledge.

3.5.2 Social Turn in Mathematics Education

These research papers show the breadth and depth of research done in the field of ethnomathematics over the past 10 years, as they place mathematics within a social, cultural, and historical context, thus supporting the view that ethnomathematics can be regarded as a reflection of a social turn in mathematics education.

Theoretical frameworks about the social origins of knowledge that began to appear in mathematics education literature toward the end of the 1980s were referred to as the social turn in mathematics education research. This approach signaled the emergence of theories developed by a mathematics education research community that has come to view meaning, thinking, and reasoning as products of diverse social activity (Lerman 2000).

This philosophical orientation coincides with humanistic and democratic concerns of many educators and researchers. The introduction of ethnomathematics by D'Ambrosio has "played a large part in creating an environment that was receptive to the social turn" (Lerman 2000, p. 24). This framework allows mathematics educators to ask questions, discuss, and create views that challenge conventional notions about the nature of mathematics.

Many of such views which reflect the social turn in mathematics education were covered in the papers surveyed by the authors of this chapter and may be framed around the interconnected ideas presented in the following sections.

(a) Mathematics is a social and cultural product

Mathematics is a human creation and mathematizing is often a deeply locally situated endeavor (Turnbull 2000). This is a reflection, indeed a confirmation, that mathematical knowledge is "irremediably social" (Beckford 2003, p. 308). Therefore, mathematical objects are viewed as inventions and dependent entities that exist a priori waiting to be discovered. Since mathematics is considered a social and cultural product, a mathematical object is embedded in and embodies different worldviews (Restivo 1994).

(b) Mathematical contributions from both the Western and non-Western civilizations

The growth of mathematics as an academic field has been nourished by the many contributions from non-Western/non-European societies (Joseph 1991). D'Ambrosio (2000) likens the production of knowledge to a great river shored up by its tributaries, water from the tributaries being the contribution of many diverse non-Western peoples, cultures, and societies. This parallels the development of Western science, which is also an assemblage of knowledge (Turnbull 2000). However, in the process of building mathematical knowledge, many of the contributions of non-Western cultures have been rendered invisible and have been appropriated, marginalized, lost, silenced, and/or hidden by what is now referred to as Western mathematics (Joseph 1991).

(c) The existence of other forms of mathematical knowledge

There is a large variety of knowledge constructed in the context of unique worldviews and played out in different, constantly changing, and increasingly overlapping social and cultural arenas. The belief in just one universal form of knowledge cannot be justified in a world that is incredibly diverse. If mathematics is socially and culturally created and re-created, then it is likely that there are other ways of doing and thinking mathematically that have produced diverse forms of knowledge. The great river metaphor used by D'Ambrosio draws attention to the hegemony of Western mathematics and captures the idea of the universality of mathematical thought. Ethnomathematics has allowed educators to acknowledge and use cultural diversity within the classroom to highlight the amazing diversity of worldwide mathematical practices (D'Ambrosio 2006).

(d) Mathematics is political

Mathematics is no longer regarded as an innocent value-free discipline. For example, Bishop (1990) points out how mathematics is used as a tool for cultural imperialism, while Porter (1995) regards mathematics as technology of distance, as it widens the gap between informal and formal mathematical knowledge. The belief that mathematics is the highest form of rational thought coupled with a rigid and intolerant way of teaching in which contestation and dissent are suppressed shows that mathematical teaching is politically influential. This approach contributes to the creation of an undemocratic and intolerant society (Hannaford 1999 apud Alangui 2010). Conversely, mathematics can be used as a productive force in the creation of a democratic and tolerant society (Zevenbergen 2001). Therefore, the mathematics curriculum needs to acknowledge the politics of mathematics education because it "is already political" (Mellin-Olsen 1987, p. 191).

3.5.3   Imperatives: Directions for Future Research

Certain imperatives have resulted from the discourse on the social turn in mathematics education, each one with the potential for providing direction to ongoing and future research projects in ethnomathematics (Alangui 2010).

The first imperative is derived from the view that mathematics is socially and culturally constructed. Thus, it is necessary to understand how power is played out in the creation and use of mathematical knowledge both at local and global levels as well as to ask which and whose worldviews are privileged in this process. For example, non-Western knowledge systems have struggled to be recognized in studies in science and technology (Eglash 2003). This is the social imperative.

The second imperative results from a need for careful analysis of what is generally thought of as the capitalist/Eastern trajectory of the development of mathematics. Thus, a critical apprehension of the growth of mathematics as a discipline could similarly dispense with the idea that it is solely a Western creation because it cannot be perceived as an imperial monolith imposed from the center to the periphery without any change or interaction.

Thus, mathematics may be thought of as a contrapuntal ensemble formed through cultural interactions and conflicts, however unequal they may have been (Tully 1995). This view of mathematical knowledge reflects the dynamics of the many capitalist/colonial encounters (D'Ambrosio 1990). It also repudiates "historiographical bias" (Joseph 1991, p. 2) against non-Western/capitalist societies, and reclaims the contributions of conquered peoples. This is the historical imperative.

The third imperative calls for the recognition, investigation, documentation, and understanding of other forms of mathematical knowledge. The challenge of this approach is to go beyond surface mathematics and dig deeper into the cultural underpinnings of the diverse ways people create complex methods and relationships in regards to quantifying objects, time, and space (Barton 1996). Respecting cultural diversity means recognizing differences as well as similarities between knowledge systems and how they interact and affect each other and how mathematical concepts and ways of thinking may help broaden our overall view of mathematics. This is the cultural imperative.

To view mathematics as political is to subject mathematics to critique, challenging the long-held view of absolute and universal truth and knowledge. Such critique diminishes the power of mathematics (Skovsmose 2000). Accepting the non-permanent, ever-changing, and evolving aspect of mathematics has deep pedagogical implications, as we are freed from an "ideology of certainty" (Borba and Skovsmose 1997, p. 17), thus allowing educators to explore a more creative and liberatory process of teaching and learning mathematics.

Mathematics helps us create conditions for democracy by developing awareness of both teachers and students through the incorporation of the social and cultural relevance of mathematical content into the curriculum and by creating a way of teaching and learning that fosters open critical dialogue between teachers and students (Hannaford 1999 cited in Alangui 2010). The extent of the contribution of mathematics and mathematics education to the creation of democratic and equalitarian societies as well as the development of critical thought among individuals remains a challenge. This imperative is both political and educational.

Some studies on the link between ethnomathematics and academic mathematics may be situated in the realm of political and educational imperatives. For example, the study conducted by Lipka (2002) revolved around the act of valuing the knowledge of elders and showing how it can be included as part of school mathematics so that diverse cultures and their unique ways of learning are not engulfed by other traditions. This project involved the documentation of knowledge and practices of elders, which led to the construction of curricular activities that connect these practices to schooling.

The study conducted by Knijnik (2002) with the MST in Brazil shows how ethnomathematics contributes in the struggle for social change by disadvantaged groups of people. In this regard, the issue is the redistribution of land through occupation, resistance, and production. This approach involves the establishment of concrete links between questions of emancipatory popular education and the processes of learning and teaching mathematics, which deal with the investigations of the:

> …traditions, practices, and mathematical concepts of a subordinated social group and the pedagogical work which was developed in order for the group to be able to interpret and decode its knowledge; to acquire the knowledge produced by academic mathematicians; and to establish comparisons between its knowledge and academic knowledge, thus being able to analyze the power relations involved in the use of both kinds of knowledge (Knijnik 1997, p. 405).

This research strategy involved the investigation of the interrelations between popular and academic knowledge in the context of specific practices of members of the cultural group. Through this approach, students "decodified and understood what the methods meant in terms of academic mathematics" (Knijnik 1997, pp. 406–408).

Such studies are significant because they involve socially, economically, and politically marginalized groups of people. The researchers reported positive outcomes in conceptual development and in making a successful bridge to academic mathematics (Alangui 2010), which showed important results in improving performance among students.

3.5.4   Concluding Remarks

The humanistic and democratic concern leading to a social view of education is consistent with D'Ambrosio's vision that ethnomathematics transforms the relationship between mathematics and society (Alangui 2010). It is a transformational endeavor with the objective of motivating active ethnomathematical work with the members of underrepresented groups.

The work conducted by ethnomathematicians, with members of distinct cultural groups in various parts of the world helps provide a basis for the recognition of diverse knowledge systems. Important contributions by ethnomathematicians to mathematics education have come to offer an arena where these members are allowed to share alternative worldviews.

This chapter has argued that the circumstances leading to the formulation of these social, historical, cultural, political, and educational imperatives are linked to one of the main goals of ethnomathematics, which is to broaden conceptions of the diverse nature of mathematics.

Chapter 4
In Guise of Conclusion

Milton Rosa and Lawrence Shirley

With the growth of ethnic and linguistically diverse student populations in schools, curricula should reflect the intrinsic, social, and cultural learning of students and teachers should be supported in their preparation to address such differences. Ethnomathematics draws from the sociocultural experiences and practices of learners, their communities, and society at large, using them not only as vehicles to make mathematics learning more meaningful and useful, but, more importantly, to provide students with insights of mathematical knowledge as embedded in diverse environments.

An important change in mathematics instruction needs to take place in order to accommodate changes in student populations. Concerns about equity in mathematics education must be at the forefront in many countries in the world. Therefore, the main goal of educators should be to accomplish equality among students, thus incorporating ethnomathematics into lessons. In this regard, mathematics has to be made equal for all students.

It is necessary that teachers emphasize connections between mathematics and other curricular disciplines and consider students' cultural backgrounds in designing and selecting mathematical activities. Students learn in ways characterized by social and affective approaches, harmony with the community, holistic perspectives, field dependence, expressive creativity, and non-verbal communication. This context enables the evolution of ethnomathematics as a research field in which one of the main goals is to link local knowledge to the mathematics curriculum by applying innovative approaches to mathematics.

In order to perceive the connection between culture and mathematics, it is crucial to underscore the importance of doing the ethnomathematical work first. This approach leads to a good understanding of the mathematical aspects of culture and a clear purpose of pedagogical activity by illustrating how mathematical ideas, procedures, and practices play a vital role in the development of human endeavors.

Ethnomathematics forms the basis for significant contributions in rethinking the nature of mathematics. This pedagogical practice is essential in developing the curricular praxis of ethnomathematics by investigating local knowledge. Thus, it is

© The Author(s) 2016
M. Rosa et al., *Current and Future Perspectives of Ethnomathematics as a Program*, ICME-13 Topical Surveys, DOI 10.1007/978-3-319-30120-4_4

necessary to broaden the discussion of the possibilities for the inclusion of eth-nomathematics and modelling perspectives which respect and give voice to the social and cultural diversity of the members of distinct cultural groups and, by so doing, develop an understanding of their differences through dialogue and respect.

In the first two decades of the 21st century, through the growth of the fields of ethnology, culture, history, anthropology, linguistics, and ethnomathematics, a greater and more sensitive understanding of mathematical ideas, procedures, and practices developed by the members of diverse cultural groups has become increasingly available. The insight from many ongoing theoretical and empirical investigations such as monographs, theses, and dissertations submitted to univer-sities in many countries demonstrate the possibility for marked internationalization of mathematical ideas, procedures, and practices expressed in distinct cultural contexts.

The increasing publication of articles, chapters, books, and news in newsletters, journals, magazines, and newspapers in many languages is an indicator of the vitality of ethnomathematics. In this context, it is necessary to highlight that the current agenda of this program is to continue its progressive trajectory to contribute to the achievement of social justice and peace with dignity for all.

In closing, this book debates few key ideas that provide for a clearer under-standing of the field of ethnomathematics and its current state of the art by dis-cussing its pedagogical actions, its contributions for teacher education, and its role in mathematics education.

References

Alangui, W. (2010). *Stone walls and water flows: Interrogating cultural practice and mathematics.* (Doctoral Thesis, The University of Auckland, Auckland, New Zealand).

Appelbaum, P., Stathopoulou, C., Govaris, C., & Gana, E. (2015). *Culture is bricks, stones and tiles randomly thrown.* Paper presented at the 67th CIEAEM conference. Aosta, Italy: CIEAEM.

Araújo, J. L. (2010). Brazilian research on modelling in mathematics education. *ZDM, 42*(3), 337–348.

Ascher, M. (1991). *Ethnomathematics: A multicultural view of mathematical ideas.* Belmont, CA: Wadsworth Inc.

Ascher, M., & Ascher, R. (1981). *Mathematics of the Incas: Code of the Quipu.* New York, NY: Dover Publications.

Babbitt, W., Lyles, D., & Eglash, R. (2012). From ethnomathematics to ethnocomputing: Indigenous algorithms in traditional context and contemporary simulation. In S. Mukhopadhyay & W. Roth (Eds.), *Alternative forms of knowing in mathematics: Celebrations of diversity of mathematical practices* (pp. 205–220). Rotterdam, The Netherlands: Sense Publishers.

Babbitt, W., Lachney, M., Bulley, E., & Eglash, R. (2015). Adinkra mathematics: A study of ethnocomputing in Ghana. *Multidisciplinary Journal of Educational Research, 5*(2), 110–135.

Barta, J., & Shockey, T. (2006). The mathematical ways of an aboriginal people: The Northern Ute. *The Journal of Mathematics and Culture, 1*(1), 79–89.

Barton, B. (1996) Making sense of ethnomathematics: ethnomathematics is making sense. *EducationalStudies in Mathematics, 31*(1), 201–233.

Barton, B. (2008). *The language of mathematics: Telling mathematical tales.* New York, NY: Springer.

Barton, B., Fairhall, U., & Trinick, T. (1998). Tikanga Reo Tatai: Issues in the development of a Maori mathematics. *For the Learning of Mathematics, 18*(1), 2–9.

Bassanezi, R. C. (2002). *Ensino-aprendizagem com modelagem matemática.* [Teaching-learning with mathematical modelling]. São Paulo, SP., Brazil: Editora Contexto.

Beckford, J. (2003). *Social theory and religion.* Cambridge, England: Cambridge University Press.

Bishop, A. (1990). Western mathematics: The secret weapon of cultural imperialism. *Race and Class, 32*(2), 51–65.

Bishop, A. (2002). Mathematical acculturation, cultural conflicts, and transition. In G. Abreu, A. Bishop, & N. Presmeg (Eds.), *Transitions between contexts of mathematical practices* (pp. 193–212). Dordrecht, The Netherlands: Kluwer.

Bishop, A. (2010). Direction and possibilities for research on mathematics and culture in relation to mathematics education: A personal view. In M. M. F. Pinto & T. F. Kawasaki (Eds.), *Proceedings of the 34th conference of the international group for the psychology of mathematics education* (pp. 337–341). Belo Horizonte, MG, Brazil: PME.

Barbosa, J. C. (2006). Mathematical modelling in classroom: A sociocritical and discursive perspective. *ZDM, 38*(3), 293–301.

© The Author(s) 2016

M. Rosa et al., *Current and Future Perspectives of Ethnomathematics as a Program*, ICME-13 Topical Surveys, DOI 10.1007/978-3-319-30120-4

Borba, M., & Skovsmose, O. (1997). The ideology of certainty in mathematics education. *For the Learning of Mathematics, 17*(3), 17–23.

Brasil (1997). *Parâmetros curriculares nacionais: matemática* [National curricular parameters: mathematics]. Brasília, DF: MEC/SEF.

Brazil (2002). *Second international congress on ethnomathematics*. Ouro Preto, Brazil: ICEm2.

Brousseau, G. (1997). *Theory of didactical situations in mathematics*. Dordrecht, The Netherlands: Kluwer.

Costa Rica (2012). *Programas de estudio de matemáticas: I, II y III ciclos de la educación general básica y ciclo diversificado*. [Mathematics study programs: I, II and III cycles of general basic education and diversified cycle]. Ministerio de Educación Pública de Costa Rica. San José, Costa Rica: MEP.

D'Ambrosio, U. (1985). Ethnomathematics and its place in the history and pedagogy of Mathematics. *For the Learning of Mathematics, 5*(1), 44–48.

D'Ambrosio, U. (1990). *Etnomatemática*. [Ethnomathematics]. São Paulo, SP, Brazil: Editora Ática.

D'Ambrosio, U. (1999). Literacy, matheracy, and technoracy: A trivium for today. *Mathematical Thinking and Learning, 1*(2), 131–153.

D'Ambrosio, U. (2000). A Historiographical proposal for non-western mathematics. In H. Selin (Ed.), *Mathematics across cultures: The history of non-western mathematics* (pp. 79–92). Dordrecht, The Netherlands: Kluwer Academic Publishers.

D'Ambrosio, U. (2001). General remarks on ethnomathematics. *ZDM, 33*(3), 67–69.

D'Ambrosio, U. (2004). Preface. In F. Favilli (Ed.), *Ethnomathematics and mathematics education (V-X)*. Tipografia Editrice Pisana: Pisa, Italy.

D'Ambrosio, U. (2006). *Ethnomathematics: Link between traditions and modernity*. Rotterdam, The Netherlands: Sense Publishers.

D'Ambrosio, U. (2007). The role of mathematics in educational systems. *ZDM, 39*(1–2), 173–181.

D'Ambrosio, U. (2009). A nonkilling mathematics? In J. E. Pim (Ed.), *Toward a non-killing paradigm* (pp. 241–270). Honolulu, HI: Center for Global Nonkilling.

D' Ambrosio, U., & Domite, M. C. (2008). The potentialities of (ethno)mathematics education: An interview with Ubiratan D'Ambrosio. In B. Atweh, A. Barton, M. Borba, N. Gough, C. Keitel, C. Vistro-Yu, et al. (Eds.), *Internationalisation and globalisation in mathematics and science education* (pp. 199–208). Dordrecht, The Netherlands: Springer.

D'Ambrosio, U., & D'Ambrosio, B. S. (2013). The role of ethnomathematics in curricular leadership in mathematics education. *Journal of Mathematics Education at Teachers College, 4*, 19–25.

Eglash, R. (1999). *African fractals: Modern computing and indigenous design*. New Brunswick, NJ: Rutgers University Press.

Eglash, R. (2003). Review of David Turnbull's Masons, tricksters, and cartographers: Comparative studies in the sociology of scientific and indigenous knowledge. *Science as Culture, 12*(1), 129–134.

Eglash, R., Bennett, A., O'Donnell, C., Jennings, S., & Cintorino, M. (2006). Culturally situated designed tools: Ethnocomputing from field site to classroom. *American Anthropologist, 108*(2), 347–362.

Eglash, R., Krishnamoorthy, M., Sanchez, J., & Woodbridge, A. (2011). Fractal simulations of African design in pre-college computing education. *ACM Transactions on Computing Education, 17*(3), 1–14.

Engblom-Bradley, C. (2006). Learning the Yup'ik way of navigation: Studying time, position, and direction. *Journal of Mathematics and Culture, 1*(1), 90–126.

Gavarrete, M. E. (2012). *Modelo de aplicación de etnomatemáticas en la formación de profesores para contextos indígenas de Costa Rica*. [Ethnomathematical application model in teacher education indigenous contexts in Costa Rica]. (Doctoral Thesis, Universidad de Granada, Granada, España).

Gavarrete, M. E. (2013). Aplicación de etnomatemáticas para la formación de profesores que trabajan enentornos indígenas. En P. Lestón (Ed.). Acta Latinoamericana de Matemática Educativa (Vol. 27, pp. 1713–1722). México, DF: Colegio Mexicano de Matemática Educativa y Comité Latinoamericano de Matemática Educativa.

Gavarrete, M. E. (2014). Elementos del conocimiento matemático cultural en la tradición indígena de Costa Rica. *Journal of Mathematics and Culture, 8*(1), 25–27.

Gavarrete, M. E. (2015). Etnomatemáticas indígenas y formación docente: una experiencia en Costa Rica a través del modelo MOCEMEI. *Revista Latinoamericana de Etnomatemática, 8*(2), 136–176.

Gerdes, P. (1999). *Geometry from Africa: Mathematical and educational explorations.* Washington, DC: Mathematical Association of America.

Gerdes, P. (2005). Ethnomathematics, geometry and educational experiences in Africa. *Africa Development, 30*(3), 48–65.

Greer, B. (2013). Teaching through ethnomathematics: Possibilities and dilemmas. In M. Berger, K. Brodie, V. Frith, & leRoux, K. (Eds.), *Proceedings of the 7th international mathematics education and society conference* (pp. 282–290). Capetown, South Africa: MES7.

Hart, L. E. (2003). Some directions for research on equity and justice in mathematics education. In L. Burton (Ed.), *Which way social justice in mathematics education? International perspectives on mathematics education* (pp. 25–50). Westport, CT: Praeger Publishers.

Herron, J., & Barta, J. (2009). Culturally relevant word problems in second grade: What are the effects? *Journal of Mathematics and Culture, 4*(1), 23–49.

Hilbert, D. (1900). Mathematical problems. *Lecture delivered at the Second International Congress of Mathematics.* Paris, France: II ICM.

Joseph, G. (1991). *The crest of the peacock: Non-European roots of mathematics.* London, England: Penguin Books.

Knijnik, G. (1997). An ethnomathematical approach in mathematical education: A matter of political power. In A. Powell & M. Frankenstein (Eds.), *Ethnomathematics: Challenging Eurocentrism in mathematics education* (pp. 403–410). Albany, NY: State University of New York Press.

Knijnik, G. (2002). Ethnomathematics: Culture and politics of knowledge in mathematics education. *For the Learning of Mathematics, 22*(1), 11–14.

Ladson-Billings, G. (1995). Toward a theory of culturally relevant pedagogy. *American Educational Research Journal, 32*(3), 465–491.

Lerman, S. (2000). The social turn in mathematics education research. In J. Boaler (Ed.), *Multiple perspectives on mathematics teaching and learning* (pp. 19–44). Westport, CT: Ablex.

Lipka, J. (2002). *Connecting Yup'ik elders' knowledge to school mathematics.* Paper presented at the Second International Congress on Ethnomathematics (ICEm2), Ouro Preto, MG, Brazil: UFOP.

Mellin-Olsen, S. (1987). *The politics of mathematics education.* Dordrecht, The Netherlands: D. Reidel Publishing Company.

Mozambique (2014). *Fifth international congress on ethnomathematics.* Maputo, Mozambique: ICEm5.

NCTM. (1991). *Professional standards for teaching mathematics.* Reston, VA: NCTM.

New Zealand (2006). *Third international congress on ethnomathematics.* Auckland, New Zealand: ICEm3.

Nunes, T. (2010). Continuities and discontinuities between informal mathematical and scientific thinking: insights for education. In M. F. Pinto & T. F. Kawasaki (Eds.), *Proceedings of the 34th conference of the international group for the psychology of mathematics education* (pp. 328–332). Belo Horizonte, MG, Brazil: PME.

Orey, D. C. (2000). The ethnomathematics of the Sioux tipi and cone. In H. Selin (Ed.), *Mathematics across culture: The history of non-Western mathematics* (pp. 239–252). Dordrecht, The Netherlands: Kluwer Academic Publishers.

Ortiz-Franco, L. (1993). Chicanos have math in their blood: Pre-Columbian mathematics. *Radical Teacher, 43*, Fall, 10–14.

Ortiz-Franco, L. (2002). The Aztec number system, algebra, and ethnomathematics. In J. E. Hanks & R. Gerald (Eds.), *Changing the faces of mathematics: Perspectives on indigenous people of North America* (pp. 237–250). Reston, VA: NCTM.

Palhares, P. (2012). Mathematics education and ethnomathematics: The connection in need of reinforcement. *Journal of Research in Mathematics Education, 1*(1), 79–92.

Petrillo, A. (1992). *Responsive evaluation of mathematics education in a community of Jos in Nigeria*. (Doctoral Thesis, State University of New York, Buffalo, NY).

Petrillo, A. (1994). *Ethnocomputers in Nigerian computer education.* Paper presented at the 31st Annual Conference of the Mathematical Association of Nigeria. Kaduna, Nigeria: MAN.

Porter, T. (1995). *Trust in numbers: The pursuit of objectivity in science and public life*. Princeton, NJ: Princeton University Press.

Rauff, J. (2009). Native American dice games and discrete probability. *Journal of Mathematics and Culture, 4*(1), 50–62.

Raussen, M., & Skau, C. (2010). Interview with Mikhail Gromov. *Notices of the AMS, 57*(3), 391–403.

Reid, C. (1996). *Hilbert*. New York, NY: Springer.

Restivo, S. (1994). The social life of mathematics. In P. Ernest (Ed.), *Mathematics, education and philosophy: An international perspective* (pp. 5–20). London, England: The Falmer Press.

Rosa, M. (2014). *Explorando saberes e técnicas locais no contexto da etnomodelagem: destacando-se as abordagens êmica, ética e dialógica*. [Exploring local knowledge and tehniques in the ethnomodelling context: highlighting emic, etic, and dialogical approaches]. (Post-Doctoral report. Faculdade de Educação. São Paulo, SP, Brazil: USP).

Rosa, M., & Orey, D. C. (2007). Cultural assertions and challenges towards pedagogical action of an ethnomathematics program. *For the Learning of Mathematics, 27*(1), 10–16.

Rosa, M., & Orey, D. C. (2010). Ethnomodelling: A pedagogical action for uncovering ethnomathematical practices. *Journal of Mathematical Modelling and Application, 1*(3), 58–67.

Rosa, M., & Orey, D. C. (2013). Ethnomodelling as a methodology for ethnomathematics. In G. A. Stillman & J. Brown. (Eds.), *Teaching mathematical modelling: Connecting to research and practice*. International perspectives on the teaching and learning of mathematical modelling (pp. 77–88). Dordrecht, The Netherlands: Springer.

Rosa, M., & Orey, D. C. (2015). A trivium curriculum for mathematics based on literacy, matheracy, and technoracy: An ethnomathematics perspective. *ZDM, 47*(4), 587–598.

Shirley, L. (2001). Ethnomathematics as a fundamental of Instructional methodology. *ZDM, 33*(3), 85–87.

Shirley, L. (2015). Mathematics of students' culture: A goal of localized ethnomathematics. *Revista Latinoamericana de Etnomatemática, 8*(2), 316–325.

Skovsmose, O. (2000). Aphorism and critical mathematics education. *For the Learning of Mathematics, 20*(1), 2–8.

Spain (1998). *First international congress on ethnomathematics*. Granada, Spain: ICEm1.

Tedre, M. (2002). *Ethnocomputing: A multicultural view on computer science*. Joensuu, Finland: University of Joensuu Press.

Tully, J. (1995). *Strange multiplicity: Constitutionalism in an age of diversity*. Cambridge, England: Cambridge University Press.

Turnbull, D. (2000). Rationality and disunity of the sciences. In H. Selin (Ed.), *Mathematics across cultures: The history of non-Western mathematics* (pp. 37–54). Dordrecht, The Netherlands: Kluwer Academic Publishers.

United States (2010). *Fourth international congress on ethnomathematic*. Towson, USA: ICem4.

Zaslavsky, C. (1973). *Africa counts: Number and pattern in African culture*. Westport, CT: Lawrence Hill Books.

Zevenbergen, R. (2001). Changing contexts in tertiary mathematics: Implications for diversity and equity. In D. Holton (Ed.), *The teaching and learning of mathematics at the university level: An ICMI study* (pp. 13–26). Dordrecht, The Netherlands: Kluwer.

Further Readings

Bishop, A. J. (2002). Research policy and practice: The case of values. In P. Valero & O. Skovsmose (Eds.), *Proceedings of the third international mathematics education and society conference MES3* (pp. 227–233). Helsingør, Denmark: Centre for Research in Learning Mathematics.

Eglash, R., Krishnamoorthy, M., Sanchez, J., & Woodbridge, A. (2011). Fractal simulations of African design in pre-college computing education. *ACM Transactions on Computing Education, 17*(3), 1–14.

Gerdes, P. (2007). *Adventures in the world of matrices*. Hauppauge, NY: Nova Science Publishers.

Lipka, J., Yanez, E., Andrew-Ihrke, D., & Adam, S. (2009). A two-way process for developing effective culturally based math: Examples from math in a cultural context. In B. Greer, S. Mukhopadhyay, S. Nelson-Barber, & A. B. Powell (Eds.), *Culturally responsive mathematics education* (pp. 267–280). New York, NY: Routledge.

Rosa, M., & Orey, D. (2013). Culturally relevant pedagogy as an ethnomathematical approach. *Journal of Mathematics & Culture, 7*(1), 74–97.

Zaslavsky, C. (1996). *The multicultural mathematics classroom: Bringing in the word*. Portsmouth, NH: Heinemann.

GPSR Compliance
The European Union's (EU) General Product Safety Regulation (GPSR) is a set
of rules that requires consumer products to be safe and our obligations to
ensure this.

If you have any concerns about our products, you can contact us on

ProductSafety@springernature.com

In case Publisher is established outside the EU, the EU authorized
representative is:

Springer Nature Customer Service Center GmbH
Europaplatz 3
69115 Heidelberg, Germany

www.ingramcontent.com/pod-product-compliance
Ingram Content Group UK Ltd.
Pitfield, Milton Keynes, MK11 3LW, UK
UKHW020216231225
466357UK00011B/173